BEXLEY
IN OLD PHOTOGRAPHS

BEXLEY
IN OLD PHOTOGRAPHS

COLLECTED BY
MICHAEL SCOTT

ALAN SUTTON
1988

Alan Sutton Publishing Limited
Brunswick Road · Gloucester

First published 1988

British Library Cataloguing in Publication Data

Bexley in old photographs.
1. London. Bexley (London Borough). Bexley,
history
I. Scott, Michael
942.1'77

ISBN 0-86299-525-6

Cover Illustration:
MANY PATHS LINKED BEXLEYHEATH WITH BEXLEY; all had to cross the River Shuttle.
This is the Pincott Fields Bridge, c. 1900.

Typesetting and origination by
Alan Sutton Publishing Limited.
Printed in Great Britain by
WBC Print Limited.

CONTENTS

HAYMAKING AT CRAYFORD.

INTRODUCTION

The London Borough of Bexley was formed in 1965 as part of the Local Government Re-organisation which combined the Boroughs of Erith and Bexley, the Urban District Council of Crayford and part of the UDC of Chislehurst and Sidcup. This amalgamation of pre-Domesday villages, Victorian industrial areas, 1930s London suburbs and 1960s new towns has not merged into one entity. Each area still has its original characteristics, exemplified by hopfields in Lamorbey, vineyards in Slade Green, silk printers in Crayford and flour mills at Foots Cray.

Famous residents of Bexley have included Lord Castlereagh, William Morris and Sir Hiram Maxim. There are Tudor buildings, Jacobean barns, Georgian mansions and the ruins of a twelfth-century abbey still to be seen and a modern shopping centre now stands beside the Roman Watling Street.

Bexley Libraries and Museums Service has a fine illustrations collection based at the Local Studies Centre at Hall Place. All the photographs in this book come from this collection: it continues to grow every year, perhaps a postcard one day, 500,000 negatives from a local newspaper the next. Each picture added is a further piece in the jigsaw that is the history of our Borough.

To all those people who have donated pictures over the years I send my thanks.

Michael Scott
Local History Librarian
Bexley Libraries and Museums Service

DENNIS'S BUTCHERS SHOP and cottage taken from the Bexley Mill. *Circa* 1930.

SECTION ONE
Roads

KNOLL ROAD, Bexley c. 1880–90.

ST MARY'S CHURCHYARD, Bexley, with the Bexley Tithe Barn in the background. The barn was demolished c. 1910.

PARKHILL ROAD, Bexley, looking west from St John's Church. Marl House is on the right, 1915.

JOYDEN'S WOOD in 1915. This extensive woodland separated Bexley, Dartford and Wilmington.

BRIDGEN VILLAGE and the Blue Anchor Pub, c. 1900.

THE NORTH CRAY ALMSHOUSES were built by the Revd Hetherington in 1771 and consisted of three homes for the poor, one for the parish clerk and the one under the clock for the school teacher. The brick building in the foreground was the infants school built in 1859.

THE JUBILEE COTTAGES in North Cray.

FOOTS CRAY HIGH STREET in 1910.

14

HIGH STREET, Foots Cray. The sixteenth-century Tudor cottages are on the right.

STATION ROAD, Sidcup.

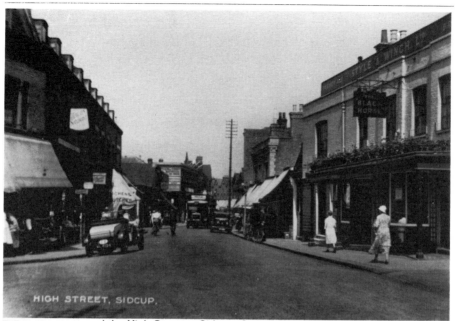

THE BLACK HORSE and the High Street at Sidcup. Style & Winch were brewers in Maidstone.

HIGH STREET, Sidcup. In 1918 the fourth shop on the right was used as a soldiers' rest room.

THE OLD POST OFFICE AND OLD BLACK HORSE in Halfway Street in 1913. The Old Black Horse
dates back to the eighteenth century, the present building to the beginning of this century.

THE OVAL at Blackfen was built in the 1930s as part of the Marlborough Park estate and consequently made shopping easier for the inhabitants of this new area.

MARKET PLACE, Bexleyheath, c. 1910. The Market House and the Pincott Memorial can be seen in the background.

AERIAL VIEW OF OAKLANDS ROAD showing the old steeple of the Chapel of Ease and the graveyard. When Christ Church was consecrated in 1878 the Chapel of Ease was demolished; the steeple, however, was only 17 years old so it was decided to leave it to serve as a mortuary chapel. As a parishioner said 'I once knew the old church without a steeple and I have lived to see the steeple without a church.'

CROOK LOG, the site of the toll gate on the New Cross Turnpike Road.

BARNEHURST ESTATE.

THE BARNEHURST RAILWAY STATION was opened on 1 May 1895 to serve the community at North Heath. It took its name from the landowner Colonel Barne. The Barnehurst estate quickly grew up around it.

THIS AREA WAS KNOWN AS HILLS AND HOLLOWS. A station, named after the landowner Colonel Barne. was opened on the Bexleyheath line to serve the community. Houses grew up round the station and a new town came into being.

WITH THE COMING OF THE RAILWAYS and later the suburban expansion from London, Bexleyheath, Welling and Sidcup turned from fields of corn into fields of houses. One developer was New Ideal Homesteads Ltd., here advertising its Penhill Park Estate at Blackfen, built in the early 1920s.

LONDON ROAD looking towards Crayford with the chimney of the tannery rising over the town.

LONDON ROAD, Crayford, looking towards Bexleyheath. Sweets was on the corner of Maxim Road, c. 1903.

HIGH STREET, Crayford.

IRON MILL LANE, C. 1917.

THE OLD ROAD was built as a detour from the original Roman road to pass the church and eventually the High Street. The One Bell public house is reported to be over 400 years old.

THE ROYAL CHARLOTTE, Station Road, Crayford.

CRAYFORD BRIDGE AND BRIDGE HOUSE. In 1907 the police box on the left was smashed by a steam lorry belonging to Cannon & Gaze. The policeman managed to get out in time!

8 - 8 - 05.

LONDON ROAD in 1905. The clock was added to a sewage lift in 1902 to commemorate the coronation of King Edward VII. The factory on the right is Vickers and the chimneys were part of the tannery.

CRAYFORD BRIDGE and waterside in 1951.

THESE ALMSHOUSES IN IRON MILL LANE were built in 1866 for the poor of the parish.

DARTFORD CREEK signified the border between Slade Green and Dartford. Here the River Cray and the River Darent join the Thames.

HIGH STREET, WELLING, c. 1920.

BELLEGROVE ROAD, Welling.

MONKS POOL. Situated at Okehampton Crescent Corner, now known as Lodge Lane. Once well-known for its watercress beds.

ST MICHAEL'S CHURCH in Upper Wickham Lane, East Wickham.

THE HUTMENTS at East Wickham were built during the First World War for those people working in munitions at Woolwich.

HIGH STREET, Erith, looking towards the Cross Keys and the White Hart.

RIVERFRONT AND CAUSEWAY, High Street, Erith, c. 1900.

CANNON AND GAYE'S STEAM MILL in the High Street, Erith, c. 1930.

PIER ROAD, Erith. Gas for the town was supplied by the West Kent Gas Company until 1910 when it merged with the South Suburban Gas Company. This photograph was taken soon after the merger.

A RAILWAY RAN FROM THE BALLAST PITS TO THE WHARF crossing West Street at this point. This photograph was taken c. 1910.

THE RIVERSIDE at Erith. In the background can be seen the deep-water wharf.

HIGH STREET, Erith, looking towards Cannon & Gaze's mill. The mill was built in 1903 to replace one destroyed by fire; it was demolished in its turn in 1937. Next to the Yacht Tavern can be seen the distinctive oil jars of George Mence Smith's.

F.•ERITH. BEXLEY ROAD. NORTHUMBERLAND HEATH.

NORTHUMBERLAND HEATH was developed at the turn of the century as a residential area. This is the Bexley Road leading into Erith.

NUXLEY ROAD, Belvedere, looking toward All Saints Church 1885.

STATION ROAD, Belvedere, looking towards the railway station. The donkey is tethered to the attractive wrought-iron public convenience.

Churches

ST MARY THE VIRGIN, Bexley, c. 1883. The church is mentioned in Domesday Book and there is evidence of the early twelfth-century architecture in parts of the building. The church has an unusual shingled roof.

ST JOHN'S CHURCH, Parkhill Road, Bexley, 1900. The church was built in 1881 to serve the growing population in the town caused by the coming of the railways to Bexley in 1866.

THE ORIGINAL STRICT BAPTIST CHAPEL in Bourne Road, Bexley, was opened in 1846. The building is now a shop.

THE CHURCH OF ST JAMES at North Cray was founded in Saxon times. This building, however, dates from the nineteenth century.

FOOTS CRAY. It is thought that there has been a place of worship here since before the Conquest. The present All Saints Church is a nineteenth-century building, but does at least possess a Norman font.

SIDCUP BAPTIST CHAPEL AND PUBLIC HALL in Hatherley Road, Sidcup.

LAYING THE FOUNDATION STONE of Christ Church, Sidcup, 26 May 1900.

ST JOHN'S CHURCH, on Sidcup Green, was built in 1885 and looked like this until 1901 when the second tower was demolished in order to enlarge the church.

ST PAULINUS CHURCH stands high up overlooking Crayford on a site that has been used for worship for over a thousand years. The present church dates from 1100 and it was popular with pilgrims on their way to Becket's tomb at Canterbury. Their gifts made the church rich and enabled it to be enlarged and improved.

ST AUGUSTINE'S CHURCH, Slade Green.

ALL SAINTS CHURCH, Belvedere, was erected by Sir Culling Eardley of Belvedere Park. The church was dedicated on 20 October 1853.

LONDON CITY MISSION in Mill Road, Erith, c. 1909.

ST JOHN THE BAPTIST CHURCH, Erith, was rebuilt in 1877. Possible traces of Roman material were found in its original fabric. A Saxon church was almost certainly on this site, despite the absence of reference to it in Domesday Book.

THE STRICT BAPTIST CHAPEL in Bexleyheath Broadway. The building bears the date 1823.

THE FIRST ANGLICAN CHURCH ON BEXLEYHEATH was built in 1835. It was called the Chapel of Ease and the foundation stone was laid by the Archbishop of Canterbury amidst great celebration. A spire was added in 1851.

SECTION THREE

Agriculture

THE BEXLEY TITHE BARN. The local vicar had a right to a tithe or tenth of each person's produce. This was stored in the Tithe Barn.

TOM COLYER AND HIS FAMILY at their farm in Bexleyheath.

HARRY PEASE farmed at Crayford and Belvedere and dealt in soft fruits. The baskets, called pecks, would hold 10–12lb. of the fruit.

EAST WICKHAM FARM HOUSE seen in 1920, with Mr Gibson by the pond.

A LOAD OF CABBAGES ready for market on Mr Gibson's farm.

A PLOUGHING MATCH on Mr Gibson's farm at East Wickham. Mr Gibson's ploughman Jack Hills is working a three-horse team and balance plough.

COMING HOME FROM MARKET 1909

MR WOOD'S TRACTION ENGINE AND TRAILER photographed at the ploughing match.

FURNER BROTHERS grew grapes at their Nursery Gardens at Slade Green.

A GROUP HOP-PICKING in the field in Longmeadow Road, Sidcup. Hop vines were very prickly and the ladies wore heavy dresses to protect themselves.

BEXLEY AND BEXLEYHEATH were ideally placed for the London markets and consequently soft fruit and specialist vegetables were grown in this area. The produce was taken by train up to the market in Borough High Street. The so-called 'Strawberry Train' is shown here in 1905.

A STEAM TRACTION ENGINE and threshing machine at Mr Humphrey's farm at Bexley.

L.W. NEWMAN founded a butterfly farm in Salisbury Road, Bexley, in 1905. Here he bred moths and butterflies for purchase by collectors.

THE BUTTERFLIES were bred in large muslin bags covering the plants on which the insects fed.

L.W. NEWMAN died in 1949 and the business was continued by his son L. Hugh Newman. Newman supplied butterflies for Winston Churchill's house at Chartwell and for the Festival of Britain.

SECTION FOUR

Industry

HALL PLACE MILL, 1915.

HORSE AND RIDER in the mill stream at Bexley.

DOUG HOLLAND'S FORGE at Sidcup.

BEADLE BROTHERS from High Street, Bexley, and their float in the Bexley Gala procession.

BEXLEYHEATH, like any growing area, needed a ready supply of bricks and the Crayford area had several brickworks.

BUILDER'S WORKMEN from Sidcup.

THE WORKMEN, WOMAN AND CAT from Stone's Boatyard at Erith, c. 1905.

EASTON AND ANDERSON'S IRONWORKS, the first manufacturing industry in Erith. The firm made pumping engines until 1904. This photograph dates from 1870.

ERITH COAL WHARF C. 1930.

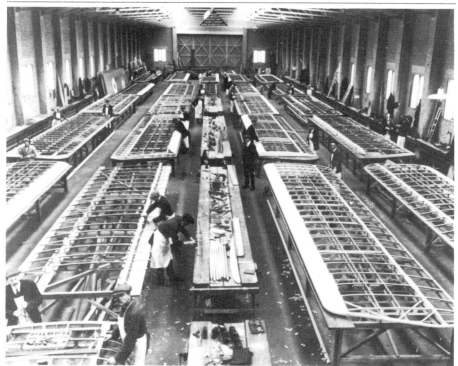

THE MAIN PLANE ASSEMBLY SHOP at Vickers Ltd., Crayford, during the First World War.

MUNITION WORKERS at Vickers in 1916.

HANDBLOCK PRINTING at David Evans & Co. Ltd. in 1955. David Evans came to Crayford in 1843 and the company is still involved in silk printing today.

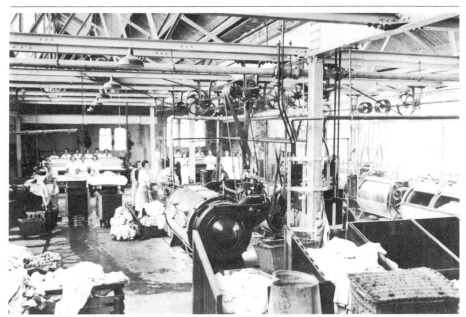

BEXLEYHEATH LAUNDRY.

A MAXIM GUN on public display at Baldwyn's Park in 1895. Hiram Maxim used to give public demonstrations with this weapon and is said to have fired corks around a public hall with it.

SIR HIRAM MAXIM, seated centre, experimented with a naphtha powered aircraft at his home at Baldwyn's Park. In 1894 members of the Aeronautical Society of Great Britain witnessed a demonstration of his machine.

Shops and Shopping

AT CHRISTMAS, butchers would buy the prize-winning animals from the London stock shows and would exhibit the carcase complete with prize winners' certificates. What a reward for being best in show! This is Wallace's Butchers at Sidcup in 1905.

YOUNG'S THE BUTCHERS in Crayford High Street decorated for the Christmas market.

ONE OF A CHAIN OF CAVE AUSTIN STORES in Sidcup High Street. This photograph was taken just before Christmas when the store was advertising Tom Smiths Crackers.

HOME & COLONIAL'S GROCERY STORE at the Market Place.

PENNEY, SON & PARKER came to Bexleyheath in 1876. The owners of the store advertised a free delivery service within ten miles and boasted that they were 'Importers and distributors of the finest provisions'.

MAY PLACE DAIRY FARM c. 1905.

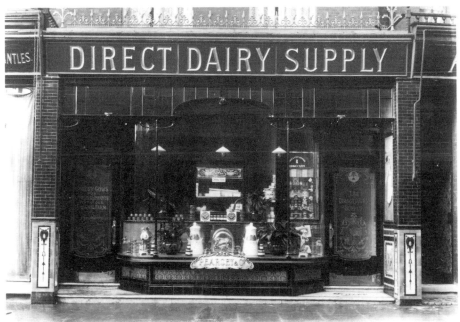

PEARCEY & CO'S DIRECT DAIRY SUPPLY in Sidcup High Street. The shop advertises 'Jersey Cows for Invalids and Infants kept at our Frognal Farm'.

SHOPS IN BEXLEY ROAD, Northumberland Heath, c. 1912.

JEVONS VILLAGE STORE at North Cray. This building was demolished in 1968 to make way for a road-widening scheme. On inspection it was found to be a Medieval Hall House. It was removed and subsequently rebuilt at the Weald and Downland Open Air Museum.

THE WELLING BRANCH OF THE ROYAL ARSENAL CO-OPERATIVE SOCIETY was opened in 1902. This photograph was taken in 1932.

HIDES STORE on the Broadway, Bexleyheath, with their Christmas illuminations in 1931.

THIS FIRM IN SIDCUP HIGH STREET advertised, in 1898, 'Hats and bonnets trimmed by experienced hands free of charge'.

GEORGE IRVING fancy goods shop in Sidcup.

C.J. COCKERELL & SONS shop at Sidcup station. The firm held a Royal Warrant from Queen Victoria and the coal wagon bears the royal Coat of Arms.

GREEN'S IRONMONGERS at the Golden Lion, Bexleyheath.

GEORGE MENCE SMITH lived at Stanley House on the heath and his ironmongery empire grew from here. His shop sold tin baths to fit everyone and an attractively priced range of coal scuttles.

AN IMPRESSIVE ARRAY OF TOOLS on display in Straws of Bexleyheath in 1934.

MRS CHALLIS at her stall in Erith High Street. Some of the brand names are no longer familiar; Oxydol, Rinso and Sunlight Soap.

MR W. HURST, hairdresser, of Bexleyheath, 1934.

WILLIAM COURT'S DINING ROOMS in Bexley Village c. 1929.

THE COSY CORNER CAFÉ near Lion Road, Bexleyheath in 1930.

CROOK LOG LIBRARY at Howell House on the Broadway.

JENKINS' LIBRARY in Bexleyheath Broadway. The shop operated a library where for a small fee the latest novels could be borrowed. The founder of the firm also founded the *Bexleyheath, Dartford & Erith Observer* in 1867 and this was printed here.

THIS POST OFFICE BUILDING in the Broadway, Bexleyheath, dated from the 1870s and was replaced by a larger building in 1937.

THE DECORATIVE ARCH to the new Marten's Grove Estate. Buy a home for £1 down, 13s. 9d. per week!

ALBERT LESTER-CLARKE'S GARAGE in the High Street, Welling, c. 1930.

'Signs secure sales. Whittle's the Sign People, Manufacturers of Signs for every purpose. 175, Broadway, Bexleyheath.' A 1929 advert.

RICHARD'S CLOCK TOWER GARAGE occupied the Bexleyheath Market House, built in the 1830s for John Smith of Blendon Hall. The Market House has also been used as a mineral water factory and a Sunday School. This photograph was taken c. 1931.

SECTION SIX

Houses

HALL PLACE is a part-Tudor, part-Jacobean house. It is a grade I listed building and now the headquarters of the Library and Museums Service.

HALL PLACE — front view, taken when the house was occupied by the Countess of Limerick.

GREAT HALL at Hall Place, c. 1920. The furniture belonged to May, Countess of Limerick. On her death in 1943 the entire contents of the house was sold and the proceeds helped to rebuild Coventry Cathedral.

DANSON HOUSE was designed by Sir Robert Taylor for Sir John Boyd and was completed in 1768. Here it is decorated for the coronation in 1953.

NORTH CRAY PLACE in 1920. This was a late nineteenth-century house. The land was occupied in 1953 as a public open space and the house demolished in 1962.

SIDCUP PLACE, seen here floodlit for the coronation of George VI in 1937, was built by an army engineer officer in 1743 in the form of a star-shaped fort. It was later occupied as council offices by the Chislehurst and Sidcup UDC.

THE MANOR HOUSE on Sidcup Green was built in 1790. This interior photograph was taken in 1944.

FOOTS CRAY PLACE was a fine Palladian mansion built in 1754. The most distinguished owner was Nicholas Vansittart, Chancellor of the Exchequer in 1812, who, in 1823, became Lord Bexley, the only man ever to hold that title.

LORD WARING outside his house, Foots Cray Place. Lord Waring died in 1940 and the house was destroyed by fire in 1949.

Howbury Moat House, near Bexley Heath.

HOWBURY MOAT HOUSE at Slade Green was built in the seventeenth century. One of its owners was the famous Admiral Sir Cloudesley Shovel.

BELVEDERE HOUSE, an early eighteenth-century building used, from 1865 to 1959, as the Royal Alfred Merchant Seamen's Institution.

LORING HALL, North Cray, the home of Lord Castlereagh and where he committed suicide in 1822.

CRAYFORD MANOR, an early nineteenth-century building in the Italian style, is the latest of a series of houses on this site.

MARTENS GROVE, Barnehurst.

THE RED HOUSE was built in 1859 by Philip Webb for his friend William Morris. Morris, one of the finest English poets and designers, lived here from the time of his marriage to Jane Burden in 1859 until 1865.

SECTION SEVEN

Public Services

THE OPENING OF THE CLOCK TOWER at Bexleyheath, July 1912. This was built at a cost of £590 to commemorate the coronation of George V.

THE PROCLAMATION OF GEORGE V at Erith in 1910.

ERITH URBAN DISTRICT COUNCIL WATER CART. Water was sprayed on the roads to help lay the dust.

DANSON PARK was purchased by Bexley UDC in 1924 for £16,000. In 1925 HRH The Princess Mary opened it to the public.

ERITH CHARTER DAY, 28 September 1938.

LORD CORNWALLIS AND ALDERMAN A.K. FRANKLIN in Danson Park for the granting of Borough status to Bexley in 1937.

THE PROCLAMATION OF THE ACCESSION OF HM QUEEN ELIZABETH II in Bexleyheath Broadway, 1952.

EDWARD HEATH, a local MP since 1950, unveils a plaque at Bexley Social Services Hall, 1961.

BEXLEY COTTAGE HOSPITAL in Upton Road early in the First World War.

THE TWELVE-BED ERITH COTTAGE HOSPITAL opened in 1875 in a villa in the High Street. The hospital moved again in 1924.

NATIONAL SCHOOL, Bourne Road, Bexley, c. 1925. The school was built in 1834 and superseded a room used in St Mary's Church.

BEXLEY NATIONAL SCHOOL, C. 1905.

EMPIRE DAY in Sidcup in the 1920s.

NEEDLEWORK CLASS at West Street School, Erith, in 1912. The school dated back to 1871 and was enlarged in 1901. The school closed in 1986.

PT CLASS at the Central School, Church Road, Bexleyheath in 1923.

GIRLS GARDENING CLASS at Burnt Oak Lane School, Sidcup 1937.

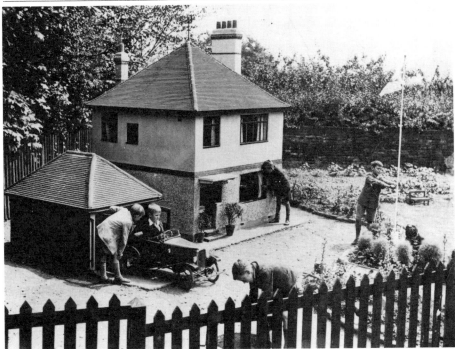

THE TOM THUMB HOME was built by children at the Crayford Junior Church of England School in 1936. It was built in one-third size and was designed to bring in every section of the school curriculum.

MECHANICAL SCIENCE LESSON at the Erith Technical College, c. 1922.

THE BELVEDERE POLICE STATION was built in 1879 at a cost of £3,386. A new building was opened in 1968.

ERITH POLICE STATION was built at Back Lane in 1845. It was replaced by a larger building on the river in 1908 to accommodate the River Police as well as the local force.

THE SIDCUP POLICE FORCE, c. 1900. The complement was a station sergeant, 3 sergeants, 2 acting sergeants, 2 mounted patrols and 17 constables. The gentleman on the left was the police surgeon. The men are wearing their winter uniform with the helmet plate bearing the Victoria or Queen's crown.

POLICE PATROLMAN SAMUEL FREDERICK YOUNG died in April 1909 after a short illness. He received a full police funeral, seen here passing Trinity Baptist Chapel in the Broadway.

THE SIDCUP FIRE ENGINE outside the Foots Cray Council Offices at Main Road, Sidcup.

ENGINEER SMEED'S FUNERAL July 1913. Smeed was an original member of the brigade, joining in May 1869. He became engineer in 1893 and served until his death aged 71.

THE BEXLEYHEATH VOLUNTEER FIRE BRIGADE was formed by public subscription in 1869. This engine, a Shand Mason, was bought in the 1880s and housed in Allen's Yard near Lion Road in the Broadway.

ERITH FIRE BRIGADE outside the headquarters at Erith Recreation Ground, c. 1900.

SECTION EIGHT

Transport

BOATS AT THE BALLAST WHARF at Erith.

A LIGHT GIG probably used by a doctor in Sidcup.

TWO HORSE AND CARTS, outside Parris the florists near Crook Log.

THE FIRST STEAM WAGON IN BEXLEY at Bexley Mill in 1902.

NATIONAL STEAM OMNIBUS at the Kings Head, Bexley.

TROLLEYBUS at Bexleyheath Clock Tower c. 1936.

THE FIRST TRAMCAR to run from Northumberland Heath to Erith, 26 August 1906.

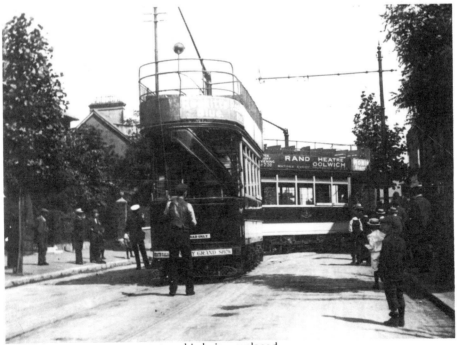

THIS TRAM HAS JUMPED THE TRACKS and is being replaced.

BEXLEY TRAMWAYS were opened in 1903 with a tramway depot built behind the Council Offices on Watling Street. The last tram ran on 23 November 1935.

BEXLEYHEATH TRAM outside the Lord Bexley.

TRAM AT BARNEHURST in 1933.

INTERIOR OF A TRAM at the Bexleyheath depot in 1930.

VIEW FROM THE GASWORKS ON CRAYFORD HILL, 1934.

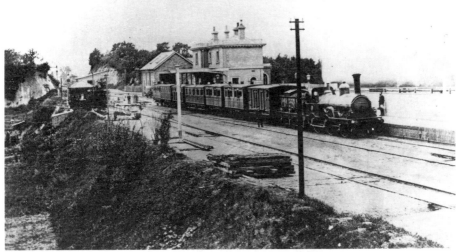

ERITH STATION was opened on the 30 July 1848. This photograph was taken in 1876.

PEMBROKE ROAD LEVEL CROSSING at West Street looking towards St John's Church.

NAVVIES EXCAVATING THE BEXLEYHEATH LINE.

A STEAM SHOVEL used on the Bexleyheath line.

WELLING STATION was opened in 1895. This photograph was taken just prior to the opening.

BEXLEYHEATH STATION, 1933.

Pubs

THE KING'S HEAD INN, Bexley Village, is first mentioned in a Hearth Tax Return of 1662. Part of the original building is still present within the pub as it is today. In 1814 a meeting was held here to discuss the enclosure of Bexley Heath.

THE BLUE ANCHOR at Bridgen dates back at least to 1825. It was known locally as the Snake and Pickaxe because of its anchor inn sign. This building was replaced by a new pub on the opposite side of the road and demolished in 1934.

THE CROOK LOG was in the list of public houses on Watling Street printed by the New Cross Turnpike Trust in 1738. For a while in the nineteenth century the inn was known as the Fox and Hounds. This photograph was taken in 1910.

THE GEORGE PUBLIC HOUSE, Bexley Village. Bert Livett was the publican here from 1915 to 1924.

THE KING'S HEAD, in the Market Place, c. 1907. The pub has recently been demolished.

THE LORD HILL at Bexleyheath was possibly named after Rowland Hill, first Viscount, who was one of Wellington's generals in the Peninsular War. The pub can be traced back to 1824 when an apprenticeship indenture was signed there. B.C. Bird was the licensee in 1907 and the horse-bus service to Woolwich started from here.

THE ROYAL OAK at Danson can be traced, as a beer shop, back to 1837, and in its present guise to 1863. It is better known as the 'Polly Cleanstairs', the name being thought to refer to a house-proud woman who once lived here.

THE LORD BEXLEY ARMS was named after Nicholas Vansittart, the first Lord Bexley, who died in 1851. This photograph was taken c. 1873 before the pub was rebuilt. The pub was pulled down in 1979 to make way for a shopping development.

THE BEAR AND RAGGED STAFF in Watling Street at Crayford, c. 1929. The pub takes its name and sign from the arms of the Earl of Warwick.

A GROUP FROM BELLEGROVE LABOUR CLUB AND INSTITUTE preparing for a charabanc outing in 1920.

THE WHITE HORSE is the real name of this pub at East Wickham, but is known by its nickname of 'Fanny on the Hill'. Legend has it that Fanny would signal to Dick Turpin when the Revenue Men were away and consequently it was safe for him to approach. Another legend concerning Turpin says that he jumped his horse over the gates of Hall Place – they are 18 feet high in the middle!

THE NAG'S HEAD at Welling dates back to 1837. It was originally the post house on the Dover Road for the whole parish, the usual place for changing horses after the coaches had left London for Rochester or Dover.

THE WOODMAN, Blackfen. This building was pulled down in 1932 and replaced by the present public house. Reffell's Brewery was the local brewery in Bexley village.

THE RAILWAY TAVERN at Sidcup in 1902 decorated for the coronation of King Edward VII. Today the pub is called the Alma.

THE SEVEN STARS PUBLIC HOUSE at Foots Cray, c. 1910. This had been an important staging inn on the main London to Maidstone Road.

THE EARDLEY ARMS at Belvedere. *c.* 1910. The pub takes its name from Sir Culling Eardley and the present building dates from the late nineteenth century.

DUKE OF NORTHUMBERLAND public house, Northumberland Heath, *c.* 1953.

ERITH, for a short while, gained fame as a riverside resort and a pier and hotel were built in 1842. This was celebrated in a rhyme about another Erith attraction, the Arboretum:

At the Pier Hotel they'll serve us well
No other house can beat them –
So we will dine and take our wine
At the Erith Arboretum.

THE BLACK HORSE, Sidcup High Street, 1897.

SECTION TEN

Sport and Entertainment

ICE-HOCKEY on the lake at Lamorbey.

BELVEDERE UNITED QUOIT CLUB.

BEXLEY CRICKET CLUB was formed in 1805. This is the youth side in c. 1866.

A TEAM OF EIGHTEEN ERITH MEN played a team including nine members of the Australian touring side in 1890. The match was drawn.

TENNIS AT HALL PLACE.

THE DANSON LAWN TENNIS CLUB enjoyed its heydey in the 1920s and 1930s when several well-known tennis stars played at the club.

MARTENS GROVE was opened as a public park in 1933. A pool was opened in 1935 when this photograph was taken and enlarged in 1939. The new pool measured 100 feet by 35 feet with sunbathing terraces and café.

ONE OF THE NEW HOUSING ESTATES to grow up between the wars was called Falcon Wood. The shopping centre boasted a children's paddling pool, photographed here in 1939.

ERITH TOWN REGATTA was initiated in 1886 and in 1900 the Erith Yacht Club was formed. By 1904 the club had over 250 members. The Regatta was held annually and in 1932 the crew from the Trafalgar public house in West Street won the 'fours'.

J. GRAHAM, the first local man to win the Doggett Coat and Badge, in 1908. This race, for watermen, was instituted by Thomas Doggett in 1715.

TO CELEBRATE THE DIAMOND JUBILEE OF QUEEN VICTORIA, in 1897, the Tradesmen's Sports and the Horticultural Show were combined to form the Bexley Gala (above and below). The gate receipts of the first show, which included a brass band competition, fire brigade competition and a very elaborate procession, totalled £121 19s. 9d.

CALLENDERS CABLES was established in Erith in 1880 and produced insulated cables for communications. During the war the factory made part of PLUTO (the Pipe Line Under The Ocean). Sir Tom Callender financed a band consisting of members of his workforce. Their fame spread and in February 1925 they made their first radio broadcast.

THE R DIVISION POLICE BAND from Woolwich.

BEXLEYHEATH TEMPERANCE BAND playing at a garden party for the employees of Mr Piggott in 1898. Mr Oldring, the founder of the band, is conducting.

MAYPOLE DANCING AT UPLANDS SCHOOL, Bexleyheath, c. 1905.

SCOUTS WITH BADEN POWELL at Foots Cray Place. Lord Waring was County Commissioner for Kent.

THE BOYS BRIGADE has always been very strong in this area of north-west Kent. This is the 14th West Kent at Bexleyheath. Members of the brigade were often seen on parade with their rifles.

ST MICHAEL'S, EAST WICKHAM, Childrens Church Guild.

TEA IN THE GROUNDS OF SIDCUP PLACE. The sailor suit for little boys was popular in Victorian times, but not necessarily with the little boys.

LOCAL BEXLEYHEATH FARMERS AND THEIR WORKERS on their annual outing, on this occasion to Woolwich.

THE BUILDING FIRM OF STEBBINGS & PANNETT of Sidcup on an annual outing.

BOSTALL WOODS were acquired by the London County Council and officially opened in 1891. The group in the middle are druids.

A WEDDING GROUP taken by the Sidcup photographer Alfred Dewey.

SANGER'S CIRCUS at Bexleyheath Market Place, 1880s.

A FAIR AT BOSTALL HEATH.

VISIT OF SEQUAH, an American quack-doctor, to Bexleyheath c. 1890. Patients went into the van and were rubbed with prairie oils for their rheumatism while the band played to drown the groans. When they came out their sticks were broken and they seemed much better, but the cure did not last. After a week the Sequah left with a torchlight procession in his honour.

A MINIATURE TRAIN used to run around the lake at Danson giving rides to children. It was opened in 1942 as part of the 'Holiday at Home' Scheme.

THE PRINCESSES' THEATRE, a 'Palace of Pleasure', was built by Vickers for their munition workers during the First World War. It was opened by Princess Christian in 1916. On the opening bill were Miss Edith Evans and the magician J.E.N. Maskelyne. This photograph was taken c. 1917.

THE PRINCESSES' THEATRE WAS ALMOST DESTROYED BY FIRE just a few months after its opening. Happily it was rebuilt and re-opened in 1919 by the Duke of York. later King George VI.

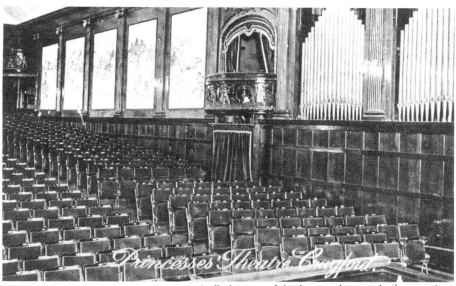

THE LUXURIOUS INTERIOR OF THE THEATRE rivalled many of the largest theatres in the country. Oak panelling, silk tapestries and green velvet seats were just part of the fittings.

THE OPENING OF THE PLAZA CINEMA, BLACKFEN on 26 July 1937. The opening was filmed for the newsreel and would have been on the Will Hay programme the next week.

THIS CINEMA WAS OPENED IN OCTOBER 1913 and soon became known as the Broadway. It was re-opened in 1928 as the 'Broadway Theatre' and again in 1932 as the 'New Broadway Theatre'. The 'Super' reconstruction was in response to the building of bigger and better cinemas, and in 1934 the Regal opened across from the Broadway. The Broadway found it difficult to compete and closed in the 1950s. The building is now a supermarket.

AN EARLY CINEMA at the Public Hall, Bexleyheath, 1913.

THE CRAYFORD FIRE SERVICE MINSTREL TROOP in February 1942.

ALFRED DEWEY was not only a well-known local photographer, but also a gifted ventriloquist. He performed locally with his lifesize dummies.

PHOTOGRAPH CREDITS

Page 68 – Sir Hiram Maxim (Science Museum).
Page 135 – Erith Pier (National Maritime Museum).